Spinning the Vast Fantastic

Vast Fa

SPINNING THE
Vast Fantastic

poems

BRITTON SHURLEY

BULL★CITY
PRESS

DURHAM, NORTH CAROLINA

Spinning the Vast Fantastic

Library of Congress Cataloging-in-Publication Data

Names: Shurley, Britton, 1978- author.
Title: Spinning the vast fantastic : poems / Britton Shurley.
Description: Durham, North Carolina : Bull City Press, [2021]
Identifiers: LCCN 2020036723 | ISBN 9781949344141 (paperback) | ISBN 9781949344226 (ebook)
Subjects: LCGFT: Poetry.
Classification: LCC PS3619.H8677 S65 2021 | DDC 811/.6--dc23
LC record available at https://lccn.loc.gov/2020036723

Published in the United States of America

Cover by Samantha Kane with Spock and Associates
Interior design by Kate Meadows with Spock and Associates

S P O C K

This book was published with assistance from the Spring 2020 Editing and Publishing class at the University of North Carolina at Chapel Hill. Contributing editors and designers were Minna Banawan, Samuel Bible-Sullivan, Dorothy Colón, Jordyn Connell, Kate Rose Dudek, London Hayes, Samantha Kane, and Kate Meadows.

Published by
BULL CITY PRESS
1217 Odyssey Drive
Durham, NC 27713
www.BullCityPress.com

TABLE OF CONTENTS

for Amelia, Thea, & Opal

When I Think I'm Through with Beauty

There's this boy who's built
like a thick brick shit-house,
    spinning a whip of forsythia

just bursting with bright
    yellow blossoms, while his

boom box floods the street
    with velvet organ chords
of old-time Baptist gospel.

    And since I was the one
who saw him, and since

    this is the poem I'm writing,
I'll say he walked so light
    he rose. That he finally lifted up.

That right there, he became
    a redbird. Better yet, the red
of a redbird's red feather

    caught up by the blue of a breeze.
Floating free from concrete

    and asphalt, from this world
that gnaws us to gristle, if we
    don't work free from its teeth.

Blessing

Today the sky's so newborn blue
        it looks like a baby's blanket.
All soft and scattered with clouds,

      so I feel like I'm swaddled and warm,
as the breeze blows light with birdsong
        through the mesh of our back screen door.

Which is all a way to say—this day
      is goddamn gorgeous. So nice I almost forget
the wreck of last week's weather. How clouds

      hunkered down in the west before one
unfurled its finger and scratched a gash
      through Oklahoma, pulling houses loose

from foundations like beets from rain-
      soaked soil. There were mothers who prayed
in bathtubs and babies plucked from trailers

      to be tucked in the shade of willows
while this storm hurled on like a train
      through some field where no one laid tracks.

But again, that's not today.
      As I said, the sky's a blue blanket.
There are breezes and birdsongs that float

      while my daughters roam wild
by our garden. One crawls through a patch of clover.
      The other picks pole beans and spinach.

If Our Daughters One Day Ask of Past Lives

We were rows
of crooked carrots

someone wrenched
from heavy clay.

We were songbirds
in spires of pines,

that dusk of hungry
crows. In a field

of black-eyed susans,
we were a thousand

black-eyed susans.
We were flies

on a deer by a road-
side, wood piled high

for a pyre. We were
bullfrogs, cicadas,

then acres of wild
alfalfa. Even now,

we're wasp and clover,
those thin moons

of dirt growing dark
beneath their nails.

Sanding

Though I know that nothing's perfect,
that children will always get splinters

and skin will bruise like fruit, I also
know I'm here—on the front porch

in August at dusk, sanding seven
kitchen cabinets to be stained and hung

next weekend. I move a fine-grit sheet
with the grain of the cabinet's oak.

Friction turning slowly to heat,
as sand rubs a rough place smooth.

With the back of my dusty hand, I retrace
each cabinet's face like my skin was young

as my daughters'. Like wood was something
new—a solid word they'll grow to need.

I've Read this Poet I Love Describe Shoveling Shit in a Pasture

How he plucked a seed from stink,
from a horse's ripe loaf of grass
           and oats, before blessing
then wiping it clean. And yes,

     he ate that seed. Which he did
as an act of love, in the heft
           of this world's bad news
that tries with its weight to drown us.

     Like the TV did last night as I watched
a man hold his sons. Both pale
           and wrapped in linen, heads
falling limp as secondhand dolls,

     when he forced them toward the camera
shouting life's clear language of grief,
           no matter the accent or tongue.
And I wish I could take

     this seed, this scene I can't unsee,
wipe it clean and bless its stench.
           But sometimes words fall short,
and nothing swallowed tastes sweet.

The Red-Winged Blackbird

Its name is a strut for the tongue.
A song that can crack the heart
    like mine did when that bird lit down

on a purpled redbud's branch
    in Ron and Kelli's field. This handful

of acres saved from an inland flood
    of McMansions drowning half of Indiana.
This field where chickens roam—

    Orpingtons, Wynadottes, Rhode
Island Reds—all hunting for bugs at dusk

    by a garden of onions and melons.
And as if that's not enough, a child's
    on his way in fall. Now I know

I know nothing for certain, but this boy
    will be born amidst magic, in a home

where cabbage, apple, and ginger
    turn to jars of kraut so crisp
my mouth wants to shout and dance.

    I hope his name holds such a tune,
that it sings like the sound of the red-

    winged blackbird and can bear
a hyphen's weight. Maybe *Banjo-*
    Nectarine or *Cannonball-Daffodil Abdon.*

Either way, his life will be music;
    he'll make this cold world swoon.

Your Heart is a Muscle the Size of Your Fist

A fistful of angry thistle that you've pulled
by a ditch along blacktop

    cutting and carving through cornfields in the
dumb, dark name of progress near
        Elkhart, Indiana. Whose name itself is elegy—
for some four-legged beast or, maybe, a day long

    gone when beauty once grew from blood to
hang like a yoke so heavy round the neck of an

    Indiana boy. His head now inked and
jarred by the size of this elk's junked heart. And who
        knows what killed that elk, if it wandered
lost and lame, limping through

    miles of meadow until it could walk
no more. Finally nuzzling the shade

    of an old-growth oak to be
pecked and pulled by buzzards so this boy would no longer
        question the girth of an elk's stilled heart. Its quick
rhythm finished, as he reached to touch

    some seed whose roots spread four old rooms
that no longer walled racket and clatter. For today, they'd

    upsprung flowers. The umber of muscle and
vibrant white petals that shone in the vast
        wide light of a sun winding round a sky. Its
axis always steady—and shining, perhaps, in excess—as that boy ran

    yelling of yarrow, how it grew so wild from a heart. Or to gather a
zinnia for seed, which he might zip tight in that thick rich soil.

To the Harvey Weinsteins et al.

Know my daughters believe in their power.
Their first-grade voodoo witchcraft
    drug back from school up the block

where they've learned this world
    and its weather is theirs to mold and control.

They've conjured inches of snow. Here, in West
    Kentucky, still two weeks shy of Thanksgiving,
where spells like this seldom work.

    But they flushed some ice down the toilet,
brushed teeth with awkward left hands,

    placed a spoon beneath their pillows,
then slept with pajamas on backwards.
    And damn, if it didn't work,

so that we could wake in a world
    slowed and stilled for a day,

our lives to be burned with abandon.
    There were cartoons, a fire, and board games;
we had pancakes and cocoa for lunch.

    And as light laid down at dusk,
the snow glowed rose in our yard.

    You should know as you wake at night,
soaked with sweat in the cold,
    these girls hold spells in their bones.

Imagine a swarm of tornadoes. Think of all
    those tender places lightning bolts could strike.

Hymn to 6th and Whatever

Where the dishwater gray of a day
got turned to rhubarb wine—

when this girl, just skin and bones,
upturned an empty crate
    and set two spoons to singing.

Her knuckle tucked loose
    between two tarnished necks

as the heels of those bowls
    began dancing; from hand to thigh
to knee, this claptrap ruckus

    of rhythm, this rumpus of metal
and flesh, calling crowds of awe-

    struck strangers like an old-time
tent revival. This herd turned true
    believers that had to tap their feet,

to add soft shimmy to hips, to grab
    a honey's hand and twirl them round

just once or twice. But isn't that
    how magic happens—a little
something spun from nothing?

    How a girl with spoons and a box
can twist us tight like tops

    then set a whole street corner
spinning. Our day abuzz
    with wonder, our hearts

all drunk and humming
    like wings in a bee-sweet hive.

For My Friend Who's Been Dreaming of Trees

Let's agree some months
seem endless, like *winter*

is a word we use for a drill
taken straight to the skull.

There's times our lives are houses
whose pipes have frozen over—

the floors all warped and feeding
a rank and moldy thaw.

But we're men in love with language,
so there's something you should know:

if you crawl from your cold in the north
to my house on the lip of the south,

there's a yellow patch of daffodils
all butter-mouthed and wild.

There's an oak whose ice-broken limbs
have buds like small hard fists.

We could make a sweet syrup from basil
to mix with bottom-shelf bourbon

and a dash or two of juice
we squeezed from an orange by hand.

Come, sit on the porch with me.
Just say the word *azalea*.

Its blooms like hearts splayed wide
for anyone passing to see.

Yellow

This color, a cousin to joy—
all brilliant and bursting its bright
    petaled stars from a hedgerow

of scraggly bushes that dance their yellow
        dance outside my daughters' window.

And they love how this yellow sways,
    when the wind blows wild as it does,
and they beg for summer to come

        so the green beneath that window
might grow to a tall yellow field.

    Sunflowers shining their yellow
each morning they wake from sleep.
    Which is not a bad dream for life,

and what pulled Van Gogh to France
        when he longed to be made anew.

Falling fast for this headstrong
    bloom whose yellow he often painted
for the blue eyes of Paul Gauguin.

        Because he lived in a yellow room
with a pair of yellow curtains

    where the yellow sun shone through.
It bathed those yellow petals,
    which sat in a yellow pot, atop

an old yellow table, until that room so flooded
        with yellow, all turned somehow to gold.

Like the pencil in a child's warm hand
	and the yellow that covers its wood
because yellow is royal in China.

	Or maybe, because each one
could write tens of thousands of words—

	an utter act of yellow magic.
And some of those words,
	I'm sure, might find a way to move us,

might pulse with a yellow that aches
	to burn though our days' thick fog.

A Little Nudge in the Crotch

Give me six better words
for spring. This season

that tickles the willy,
that stirs from snowmelt

and leaf-rot to rise
like a bright surprise.

Like I've sprawled out
wide in the yard,

talking dirty
to each green thing

for a gaggle
of girl scouts to see.

But who cares
what people think?

What they'd say
of a man overcome—

face down
and swimming wild

through the buzz
of bee-hum and henbit.

How he picks
and sniffs each blossom

or parts those orchid-
thin lips to sweet-talk

its pink and violet.
While the bee

sticks its whole head in—
wallows-wide

that flower's flute
to taste what's been missing

for months. Say a scar
on a sun-starved thigh

or a shoulder's brown
dipper of freckles,

each one licked
warm by spring.

That's what we
dream of all winter,

why we do what bees
do to blossoms.

In Case Our Daughters Still Wonder Why Poets Sing of Spring

Because there are days in May
when the heat burns off at dusk
      and you can sit on a porch and rock
by a pot that you've sown with zinnias.

You can watch the sun shimmy down,
how it dips behind the oaks, as they blur
      to dark silhouettes—some stark
and silent herd of giant grazing beasts.

And from here I'd bet you forget,
the sun's a roiling fire,
      a blast furnace waiting to dim
in a half-dozen billion years.

But that's the thing you'll forget.
Because today the light is softer,
      filled with pinks and purples,
and from the cool blue shade of our porch,

you might even say it's gentle.
This light like a quilter's hand
      threading thin sprouts from seeds
through a black patch of soil.

On a day such as this, while the sun
wanders off in the west, you might see
      how we long for light. You might sense
the smallest tug, even feel you're leaning too.

Hymn to the Bounty

Because it's hard not to be a glutton.
When you're out before noon in June
     in a West Kentucky field
bursting with dusky berries.

    Those rows and rows of bushes
so heavy and full with fruit
     their branches can't help but droop.

    Fat bees all drunk and buzzed
do their bumble from blossom
     to blossom. Tell me how
you could not pick gallons,

    not pluck big blue handfuls
straight from bush to mouth.
    Tell me how you could stop

    from stooping, from bending your back
for each berry that lay in the dirt
     at your feet, those so ripe
and plump their skin's gone thin and split.

    How could you not eat it all:
this field, these bushes, this sunlight;
    this ripeness, this bee-hum, this dust?

Spinning the Vast Fantastic

*"An Astounding Phenomenon in Kentucky—Fresh Meat Like
Mutton or Venison Falling from a Clear Blue Sky"*
— *The New York Times*, March 10, 1876

Where at 2 p.m. on a Friday, a girl can
make soap in her yard, look up

    toward a cornflower sky, and be showered
with chunks of meat. For ten long minutes
    it rains. Enough to fill a horse wagon,

old Uncle Boot might say. All, while she
    stirs in salt and lard, or leaches

white lye from ash, and listens when men
    wander past, leading their light brown mules
and weighing this mystery's merits.

    One claims it's *bushels of mutton.*
The other says *bales of venison,*

    *cut from a herd of deer that grazed
on morels and roses.* Still, Benjamin
    Franklin Ellington swears *it's the muscle*

of bears. Others think stables of horse
    meat, the lungs of slaughtered infants,

or pecks of flesh from a knife fight, picked up
    and spit from a whirlwind two counties over.
Most blame the rain on vultures. How they

    vomit if scared by a sound or when needing
to lighten their load. But this girl knows

the bellies of vultures, their circles spun
black through a sky. She knows this Friday
was blue. Clear and clean as the *o* in *wonder*.

Parthenogenesis

If the ankle of a horse is holy, then so is the cow's
cracked hoof, the sheep's bleating tongue, the wiry

gray taint of a sow. And if each of these things
is divine, who's to say God's skin can't shed?
That he can't slink back with a snake's forked tongue,

belly scratched and hallowed by gravel, to hiss or kiss
like the rest of us just dragging these bodies through Eden.

Last night, in a Louisville zoo—where north is stitched
to south and where slaves, when the sky was clear,
tried to swim the moon-bright Ohio—this virgin

python named Thelma gave birth to a clutch of eggs.
There were no shepherds or wise men,

no decrees for butchering babies. There was just
a guard on his rounds in this city so few would
call holy. His light like a star's far shine as it lit

on Thelma's coiled scales, warming what no one
expected—these things that were not, then were.

Hymn to the Moon and Peaches

Because I think of the night you and I
        were chasing that peach of a moon.
How it rose and fell while we drove
    through dimming hills of bluegrass

and hollows filled with whiskey.
        How large that ripe moon loomed.
As hills died down to fields
    of rich folks' sprawling horse farms

which laced some college town
        where boys and girls packed bars
like cattle crowd a trough.
    But the moon we were chasing

was rising. The night, as they say,
        was young, and you and I
were driving. Not that we'd grown
    too old or that we'd had our fill of whiskey;

lord, I drink like a dried up well. It's just
        this night had a moon. This moon
that we both swore was the best
    we'd ever seen, and we now knew enough

to look. So we stared at that ripe
        peach moon. Watched it hide
behind the hills, shine through stands of pines,
    then rest in the palm of the sky

like a handpicked summer fruit.
      Now I know this has all dissolved,
that it's little more than metaphor—
      that moon, the fruit, the hunger.

But if this were not a poem,
      and you and I were here, in this room
with a bowl of fruit, with a ripened summer
      peach, I swear I'd ask for nothing.

Nothing more than to sit and watch
      as the skin of that fruit parts your lips.
As your teeth sink soft through its flesh,
      as its juice drips sweet down your chin.

To Francisco Starks, Who Stole My Car from My Driveway, Late One Saturday Night

I like to think you desperately needed it.
That its missing rearview mirror
    must have spoken like a haunting past—

    some ghost on your heels like a hound
you'd love to forget exists.

I hope the smell of hay and compost,
worked through seats and floor mats,
    from loads I hauled all day
for the garden my family was planting,
    somehow called through the night like a song.

Like the song of a rare wise owl
neither you nor I could name.

And I hope the shovel you stole,
resting inside my trunk, has found
    itself a home, doing deep and dirty work
such things are made to do.

I pray you're also blessed with children,
since you stole the car seat we bought.

And that your son or daughter
has helped you, not to steal
    such things as cars, but to put
that shovel to use. Doing things
    like planting fruit—a bramble or prickly thicket

of gooseberries, blackberries, raspberries—
which have taken a quick bright liking

to every scrap of sunlight and air their leaves
have been free to breathe. Your yard over-
taken and wild, devoured by sugar and thorns.

Against the Pawning of Steel Guitars

Even if your wife is pregnant
      and the home you hope to buy
costs more than you've squirreled away.

    Even if the thing's sat silent,
sleeping like the dead might do,
      in back of a darkened closet,
in the room of a rented house
    you know you'll soon outgrow.

Because some things rise from the dead.
      Because your body's full of blood.

Now I know this talk of death,
    of blood and sleep, seems odd
on the eve of having a child.

      But, Joe, don't think I'm drinking—
not this early on a Friday morning—

    or I missed what you said that night
when you talked of a girl you know.
      A stone-cold poet, you called her.

This bird in a scarlet hijab,
    this quiet refugee just bursting with heart-
breaking song as she walked the racket
      and chatter of a high school hall in Kentucky.

I've never met this girl, but I think
    of her now as an old Polish bird.

One that sang, perhaps, to Milosz
        as he wrote that letter to Ginsberg,
sitting cold outside in his garden.

        This poem he grew to hate, you showed me
one night in a bar, with this line
        that floored us both. His life's
a discarded tire, lying by the road.

        So if two men can stand in a bar,
after drinking well past midnight,
        and one can count without slurring
on the tips of two tipsy fingers
        the times in his life he's made music—

a music that makes him weightless,
        his fingers less clumsy, his boots less heavy—

then that man should keep that guitar.
        We live in the midst of *a murderous century.*
Hold tight the things you need,
        those filled with love and song.

Another Poem in a Time of War

We gather what we need from the cupboard—
bags of flour and sugar; salt and cinnamon;

cups and spoons for measuring. I pull milk
and butter from the fridge, stir them in

with an old wood spoon. My daughters add
berries by handfuls. What could I tell them of war?

I have never plucked shrapnel
from an infant's slashed skin, never ripped

a mother's body from rubble. All I can say
is we're here, in a world I find hard to fathom,

trying not to rush the days, in this house
with a warming oven that will soon

smell faintly of cinnamon. Our counters
filled with muffins, their tops inked dark and blue.

Headless Wonder

"Miracle Mike, the Headless Chicken, was a plump, five-year-old cockerel...beheaded on 10 September 1945... [he] stuck around for a good 18 months without his head."
    —*Scientific American*

Let's say a farmer loves his wife. That his wife,
in turn, loves her mother. And this mother
    has always loved the slow-roasted neck

of chicken. Let's say she's coming for dinner.
    So this farmer walks his field, picks a fat-

necked bird, and brings the ax blade down—
    plum missing the bird's main vein and the fruit
of most its brain. Let's say this bird runs around,

    as headless birds will do. But later, it settles
down. Say it pecks the dust with its stump.
    Tries to preen its blood-specked feathers

then crows this throaty song that swells
    deep-down from his gut. Say the farmer
leaves it be. But come morning, that bird's

    asleep. His head, that no longer is,
tucked soft beneath one dark wing
    like this earth and its axis was steady.

Say the farmer now feels how it wobbles. That he
    gives that bird a name and feeds it for months
to come. Dropping water and bits of cornmeal

    down the throat of a bird crying out like a chord-
wrenched ragged hymn. This body that held
    its hunger, this ghost that refused its call.

Elegy for My Uncle, Who Kept a Jar of Arrowheads atop His Bedside Table

He must, in his youth, have waited—
    face to the screen door's rust—for summer

storms to pass, so as soon as the rain
        subsided he could bolt for fields
and pastures. Combing hay and wheat
    and corn for rain-bright stones that rose,

a moment somehow weightless,
    through that slip of southern clay.

His boots mud-heavy and red,
        his kidneys still burning their sugars,
his back not yet begging for pills,
    as the glint of some point caught his eye.

This boy whose father carved wood
    and praised the patient hand—how stones

once flaked by long-dead light
        might rise from earth to palm.
He tucked each stone in his mouth's
    soft pouch, filing its edge with his tongue.

Learning there's one taste to iron,
    little difference in soil and blood.

We Shall Have Everything We Want

after Frank O'Hara

And there'll be no more dying.
Because we'll all drink Coke
    or beer dripping sweat from the cooler-

cooled can, as the summer-long smell
    of charcoal flirts and kisses and tumbles
with the breezy sweet scent of laundry

    left to dry on a backyard line.
There'll be no more news of boys
    who steal their mothers' rifles

to gun down whole classrooms
    of children. And there'll be no more
talk about girls who are pulled

    from crowded busses and raped
on gravel streets. Let us each
    have a life we might live with.

Let us all grow dizzy with love.
    As we spin round our kitchens
with someone, while fruit simmers down

    on the stove, and our lips touch an ear
to whisper: *my field of clover in blossom,*
    song I can't cough from my throat.

Hallelujah

To the tilt-a-whirl twist and turn
    of the winding Blue Ridge Parkway,

as I dizzy in back of a car
        on this two-lane that hair-pins
and corkscrews through June-lush
    crests and swells of hills named long ago.

Because people named this ridge,
    and this name feels somehow true.

That sacred, sweat-soaked wrestle
        of head, heart, and tongue,
until we're pinned then limp along
    with the best we can do for a name.

Which is what the *Blue Ridge* is—
    a gasp to trap a marvel.

This trick of sunlight and water,
        from fog or low-slung clouds
that slink these mountains' ribs
    turning green to shades of blue.

All because water turns weightless.
    Then floats past trees and streams,

both so full of water, whether we see it
        or not. Just like the backyard tomatoes
that plump and swell in my garden
    roughly four hundred miles away.

Or these rivers of blood in our bodies,
    each salty and dark like seas

that churn this weather and wind,
      sweeping clouds through mountains
turned blue. Which is nowhere near
    the word for how I'm feeling now.

So again, I say, *Hallelujah.*

A Few Quick Thoughts on Tubers

Which sounds, I admit, like *tumors*
and must, on some long scroll of words,
    have shared a common root.

Some thick and prickly thread
    that cinched to bind them tight
like the lips of a sack's wide mouth.

    And most often, I think it's burlap.
Heavy and bursting with Carolina
    Reds, maybe dark Georgia Jets,

someone dug from sandy soil
    where they've grown and spread unseen.
Which is also what tumors do.

    Perhaps that's why I dreamed last night
of my father home from the doctor.
    We sat at an orange table

by my weed-wild backyard garden
    where I killed young rows of potatoes
with too much compost and lime.

    But here was this feast of homegrown
tubers. Peruvian purple hash with dill
    scrambled eggs. Roasted yams, pecans,

and almonds tossed in maple syrup.
    And with every plate we filled,
we ate till there was no more.

Sharing a Fifth of Bourbon with a Friend
Who Fears What Follows

Again, we've been watching the news,
how troops comb caves in a desert
    for three hundred kidnapped girls
taken for wanting to read.

    We doubt they'll ever be found.
Yet today we were out in the yard,
    building a coop for chickens, rapt
with the minor miraculous.

How a thumb on the mouth of a hose
sends barefoot and buck-
    naked children squealing
through brilliant prismatics,

    that magic of sunlight on water
as it falls toward the skin and clay
    of this yard in south Alabama.
Still, despite these blessings,

    my friend hopes *this* isn't *it*.
He wants to know there's something more,
    that somewhere some grand musician
sits at a grand piano and waits

    for our soul's last note to be played
for his grand old tune. I have no idea
    what follows. But brother, look hard at this banquet:
our table filled with love and plenty.

We've got wives and daughters and chickens,
turnips and kale from the garden.
We've got booze and backyards
and water. Who are we to beg for more?

Note to My Wife in Case I Should Die before Her

Remember Kentucky's Octobers,
    when the side of this earth we called home
tipped itself back from the sun

      and all of summer's swelter
slipped to the backs of our minds.

How we awed or gawked or reveled,
    any dumb word you might choose,

at those sunsets which came on
      spectacular, and the leaves
as they cooked off last sugars.

All the russets and scarlets of oaks;
    each hickory and poplar's gold,
and that lone young maple we planted.

      How it grew and seemed to burn—
from green to yellow then red—

every leaf like a body on fire,
    fuel for a flame that likes dancing
when the breeze up and whistles its tune.

      So my love, there's no need for a casket,
for the shovel's dull edge or a hymnal.

Fold my ashes, by hand, in the garden
    so our girls can see each autumn
as proof this world spins on.

Notes

"I've Read this Poet I Love Describe Shoveling Shit in a Pasture" references and is highly indebted to Steve Scafidi's poem "Ars Aureus" from his collection *The Cabinetmaker's Window*.

"A Little Nudge in the Crotch" takes its title from a line in Frank O'Hara's poem "[Poem] I don't know as I get what D. H. Lawrence is driving at."

"Parthenogenesis" borrows the phrase "if the ankle of the horse is holy" from Larry Levis's poem "There Are Two Worlds," from his collection *Winter Stars*.

"Against the Pawning of Steel Guitars" borrows the phrases "a discarded tire, lying by the road" and "a murderous century" from Czeslaw Milosz's poem "To Allen Ginsberg."

"We Shall Have Everything We Want" is after Frank O'Hara's poem "Ode to Joy," from his *Collected Poems*.

Acknowledgments

Many thanks to the editors and staff of the following journals in which some of these poems have appeared:

Briar Cliff Review: "A Note to My Wife in Case I Should Die before Her"

Crab Creek Review: "If Our Daughters One Day Ask of Past Lives"

Chattahoochee Review: "Headless Wonder" and "To the Harvey Weinsteins et al."

Indianapolis Review: "For My Friend Who's Been Dreaming of Trees"

Iron Horse Literary Review: "Elegy for My Uncle, Who Kept a Jar of Arrowheads atop His Bedside Table"

The Massachusetts Review: "Parthenogenesis"

Rock and Sling: "Blessing"

South Carolina Review: "To Francisco Starks, Who Stole My Car from My Driveway, Late One Saturday Night"

Southern Humanities Review: "When I Think I'm Through with Beauty"

Southern Indiana Review: "Spinning the Vast Fantastic"

Tar River Poetry: "Sharing a Fifth of Bourbon with a Friend Who Fears What Follows"

Valparaiso Poetry Review: "The Red-Winged Blackbird"

Waccamaw: "A Few Quick Thoughts on Tubers" and "Your Heart is a Muscle the Size of Your Fist"

Thanks to Noah Stetzer for always believing in this book. And special thanks to Ross White, whose eyes and ears have made these poems more lively and strong.

Thanks to Samantha Kane and Kate Meadows for making this book so beautiful.

Thanks to the Kentucky Arts Council for its financial support and encouragement through Emerging Artist Awards. And thanks to the Rockvale Writers' Colony for an idyllic space to write and revise.

Thanks to my parents, for so many, many things.

And, as always, unending thanks to Amelia, Thea, and Opal. Without you the page would be bare.

About the Author

Britton Shurley's poetry has appeared in such journals as *Southern Humanities Review*, *Hampden-Sydney Poetry Review*, and *Southern Indiana Review*. He is the recipient of Emerging Artist Awards from the Kentucky Arts Council in both 2011 and 2016 and is an Associate Professor of English at West Kentucky Community & Technical College, where he edits *Exit 7: A Journal of Literature & Art* with his wife, the poet Amelia Martens. They live in Paducah, Kentucky, with their daughters and curate the Rivertown Reading Series.